Dr. Mini Mental Health Series.

Book 3: Penelope fights Anxiety

DR. MINI TANDON

AuthorHouse™
1663 Liberty Drive
Bloomington, IN 47403
www.authorhouse.com
Phone: 833-262-8899

Because of the dynamic nature of the Internet, any web addresses or links contained in this book may have changed since publication and may no longer be valid. The views expressed in this work are solely those of the author and do not necessarily reflect the views of the publisher, and the publisher hereby disclaims any responsibility for them.

Any people depicted in stock imagery provided by Getty Images are models, and such images are being used for illustrative purposes only.
Certain stock imagery © Getty Images.

This book is printed on acid-free paper.

ISBN: 978-1-6655-1606-8 (sc)
ISBN: 978-1-6655-1605-1 (e)

Library of Congress Control Number: 2021902572

Print information available on the last page.

Published by AuthorHouse 02/09/2021

authorHOUSE®

Penelope and her parents came to the office of Dr. Mini Mental Health—a child psychiatrist...

We socially-distanced and wore our masks,

And possibly, the pandemic will pass.

But Penelope continues to worry,

Less like a light shower,

More like a heavy flurry.

School has opened, and she won't go.

Her appetite is poor, and her activities low.

When I open her door to take a peek,

She is never truly ever asleep.

At first it was just a few little things,
And then it all began—
A snowball of many worries
Of a very, very wide span.

There was

Fear of the Dark

Fear of the Rain

Fear of feeling Judged

About her Smart Brain.

Fear of Mistakes, although she still tries,
With every small error, she
Cries and she cries.

Her heart races and her hands
drip sweat, I give her towels
They feel so wet.

I worry a little, she worries a LOT...
SO tell me, Dr. Mini—
Is this something or is it NOT?

Dr. Mini and the family
discussed their thoughts:
"Because it has been over half of a year,
With so many worries and with so many fears,
So many symptoms, signs and tears...
It seems reasonable to say
Penelope has ANXIETY and
that is OK!

First there is therapy to reframe
her thoughts and to empower her
To address her "oughts".
Deep breathing and meditation
to relax her brain
To calm the storms,
During the rains.
There is also medicine if you should choose...
So please, please
Do not get the blues.
This kind of concern does not involve
a mask, there is no handwashing
But a very different kind of task.
We will work through this,
You came to the right place.
This is a journey and certainly no race."

After treatment for anxiety,
Penelope returned to school
excitedly.
She sat next to her good friend—
Willie (Wannaknow).
Willie was excited to have her back.
"I saved all your schoolwork
in a perfect stack!"
Penelope replied she was glad
he did, but she no longer
Needed them ordered
In a perfect grid.
"I am doing much better, and
I don't worry as much!
In fact, you can order my papers
in a messy bunch!"

PARENTING PEARLS

This book is not a substitute for medical care. Many clinicians, not limited to pediatricians, child psychiatrists, pediatric neurologists, psychologists, and therapists can help with anxiety and many other mental health concerns. Anxiety can be a serious illness--especially when not addressed.

In general, it involves

Intense worry about many topics

with impaired functioning,

lasting at least 6 months.

There are many types of anxiety and Generalized Anxiety Disorder (this story) is only one type.

It is treatable with therapy and/or medications.

Please seek early and appropriate mental health treatment for your child.

Best,

Dr. Mini

Printed in the United States
By Bookmasters